The

One-Minute
Jerk at Work

Rich Salon, SPHR, SHRM-SCP

(aka Rich-The-HR-Guy)

Foreword by David Saunders, Madison+Main

The One-Minute Jerk at Work

E-mail: Rich@OwnershipConnection.com

Softcover: 979-8-9855193-7-2 (ISBN)   Hardcover: 979-8-9855193-6-5 (ISBN)

E-book: 979-8-9855193-8-9 (ISBN)

Dedication

To Laura, Cory, and Mary.

My amazing family, who inspire me to take
care of others before taking care of myself.

Your dedication to our family provides motivation
for me to become the best version of myself.

CONTENTS

FOREWORD

Let's face it — we've all worked with *that* person. The one who hijacks meetings, thrives on passive-aggressive emails, disrupts the entire office with a shrieking voice or micromanages the flavors in the Keurig Coffee machine. *That* person can make every day feel like Monday.

Over the course of my career — in boardrooms, conference rooms, and newsrooms — I've encountered more than a few jerks at work. I've known quite a few **Teflon Toms** and a few **Micromanaging Marias**. I've hired **Pessimistic Petes** and fired **Billy the Bullies**.

Some wore suits, others wore name tags. Some had corner offices, others lurked in the back of the cubicle farm. But they all had one thing in common: they disrupted culture, destroyed morale, and derailed progress. And the worst part? Most of them didn't even realize they were doing it.

That's why this book, written by HR guru Rich Salon, matters.

The One Minute Jerk at Work isn't just a clever title — it's a how-to guide. How to spot jerks. How to handle them. And maybe, just maybe, how to fix those Jerks at work. This easy-to-read resource gives you 26 personas of "jerks at work." In each example, Rich identifies toxic behaviors and delivers practical strategies to deal with them. The result? Stronger teams, healthier communication, and a workplace that actually works.

This book is for professionals who are tired of walking on eggshells. It's for managers who want to lead with empathy, not ego. And it's for anyone who believes that respect, kindness, and accountability aren't outdated ideals, but essential values worth protecting.

It challenges us to take a hard look at how we communicate, collaborate, and contribute — and it does it with humor, honesty, and just enough attitude to keep things interesting. In full disclosure, I've been pieces of a few of these characters myself. The younger me had some **Arrogant Andy** in him. The older me has had shades of **Authoritarian Author** and **Potty Mouth Patrick.**

So, take a deep breath, open your mind, and maybe brace yourself a little. The truth in these pages might sting — but if you're willing to listen, learn, and grow, it just might save your team (and your sanity). Because the only thing worse than a jerk at work… is being one.

Life is too short to work with a jerk.

— David Saunders

PREFACE

Do not let jerk's rule. Instead, institute the No Jerk Rule.

- R.T.H.R.G.

What would your career feel like if you were rarely disrupted or bothered by someone's inappropriate or offensive behavior? The purpose of *The One-Minute Jerk at Work* is to help everyone currently immersed in a career work in a respectful and courteous workplace. A person can ruin your day in sixty seconds or less, but they have no right to do so. Finding and sustaining the level of satisfaction you desire is important, as this will help enable you to perform your best work. No one should ever lose sight of their instincts to capitalize on their career purpose and the things in life that are important to them. This book will inspire you to never settle working among people whose behavior is not acceptable. You will discover how you can perform your best work, even if it means helping someone overcome poor behavior.

The premise for *The One-Minute Jerk at Work* was inspired by my career as a Human Resources and Employee Relations leader in large, successful companies. It was also inspired by my two prior books, *Career Trust,* and *Unleashing Your Career.* These books address employment, empowerment, and economic issues surrounding careers and were created for everyone who draws strength and seeks self-actualization from their work. Each book also approaches the desire for work-life balance, often not the first thing we think about but one cannot deny it is what each of us craves.

I authored this book because people frequently dedicate precious work time to dealing with others who display inappropriate behavior. Based on my past roles where I was accountable for the welfare of work groups as large as 20,000 employees, there have been far too many instances where a person was able to ruin someone else's day in one minute or less, and can sometimes ruin someone's week or longer. The level of gratification someone seeks from their career should never be compromised or interrupted. Attaining an appropriate work-life balance is not easy, and having to take home needless frustrations must be minimized.

Solutions to the jerk-like behaviors discussed in this book will help you preserve a positive work experience in your journey to support yourself and your family. As "The Jerk Authority," I gain limited satisfaction in helping people turn around their unruly behavior. However, I do draw pleasure in seeing how everyone around that person finds the climate more gratifying after jerk-like behavior has been managed. As for you, if achieving your vocational dreams and making the world better is important, the insights in this book will assist in making your career a more fulfilling one.

INTRODUCTION

Surround yourself with jerks and what might you get? Fired.

- R.T.H.R.G.

This book is about the negative impacts an organization and its team members experience when working in the presence of inappropriate and offensive behaviors. The content in each chapter addresses how people feel when working alongside a "jerk" and methods to consider when dealing with offensive behavior.

Each of us needs to examine our own behavior at work, this is a given, and you are empowered to make changes within yourself when needed. However, the book's content focuses on the behavior of others around you. This includes coworkers, your superiors, and people who report to you. The content within the chapters can help you devise strategies to address and prevent unwanted conduct.

The content of this book stems from my experience as a Human Resources and Employee Relations leader. It has been my privilege to provide coaching and guidance to thousands of leaders and employees throughout my career. I have worked tirelessly supporting regions across most of the U.S. as a leader within organizations including The Home Depot, Circuit City, Penske, and Lowe's. Together, the business leaders and I typically achieved the highest level of employee engagement.

The One-Minute Jerk at Work is based on insights devoted to helping you attain the respectful environment you desire. Throughout this book, unacceptable and undesirable workplace actions will be referred to as "jerk-like" behaviors. The chapter names pair an undesirable behavior with a common first name, creating a fictitious character.

My goals for you, the reader, include:

- Commit to creating and upholding the most respectful workplace without compromise.
- Identify and address obstacles that hinder an organization's competitive edge.
- Learn how and when to transform a toxic work culture into a positive one.
- Foster a more fulfilling career by collaborating with respectful colleagues.
- Play an active role in creating a workplace where people feel valued and appreciated.

About the title - *The One-Minute Jerk at Work* - what does the word "jerk" mean to you? For me, I tend to think in terms of behavior that a reasonable person would not tolerate. It might also be referred to as inappropriate or offensive behavior. Conduct that is not welcome includes rude, condescending, obnoxious, and humiliating. Other names for "jerk" can include creeps, bullies, tyrants, weasels, or my personal favorite, "what a dirtbag."

How do you read this book? Each chapter is a separate message to help you identify and address inappropriate behavior at work. The chapters do not flow together to create a story. At the end of each chapter, you will find a "Point to Ponder" and a "Question to Consider." I hope you take a moment to reflect on the message and respond to the question.

Use this book as a source of inspiration, reminding yourself not to settle when it comes to your work experience. Read this book with open eyes as you may discover that you practice one or more of the offensive behaviors. If this occurs, take a partner to help you address this challenge. Remember, you are empowered to make changes within yourself when needed.

This book is not intended to be a Human Resources manual, nor does it contain legal advice. If at any time you observe behavior that rises to the level of being considered harassment, discrimination, retaliation, or defamation, you would be wise to contact a senior leader, Human Resources member, or legal counsel. Recognizing many workers do not have access to a Human Resources representative, the person running the office is rarely a trained HR professional. It is important to identify an appropriate person who can manage your concern. The chapters address conduct that can contribute to a toxic culture, where negative impacts include absenteeism, turnover, and reduced productivity. Each of these is avoidable.

There are no guarantees that every employment environment will remain professional since multiple variables contribute to the level of tact and diplomacy. However, by examining your happiness at work, coupled with the reality that you work about 130,000 hours over the course of your career, you should be inspired to perform your best every day. You are invited to read this book to help you reach the level of career fulfillment you seek and to help make your organization an "employer of choice."

Now, let's learn how to manage jerks before they ruin someone's day.

The Impact of Jerk-Like Behavior in the Workplace

You want to work in an environment where you can perform at your best. Considering the vast number of hours you will dedicate to work over the course of your career, it is essential to operate within a respectable environment. Offensive behavior can foster a distrustful workforce and an unethical atmosphere, leading to missed deadlines, unmet goals, and damaged credibility. Disruptive behaviors can tarnish the reputation of a department or even the organization's brand, affecting financial results, shareholder value, and the respect employees hold for their employer.

The loss of worker productivity and increased absenteeism have often been traced to the presence of inappropriate conduct. In some cases, this has resulted in the loss of top-performing employees. While every organization may experience occasional dips in customer satisfaction, when analyzing the issue, it may be due to disruptive team members.

Understanding why people exhibit jerk-like behavior is a critical part of any company's commitment to its employees. Determining whether inappropriate actions are intentional or stem from blind spots is essential. It is possible that the individual is unaware of the negative impact their behavior has on others. Numerous causes may explain these actions, including lack of training, unclear processes for resolving issues, or a workplace climate that lacks accountability. Understanding the "why" may also assist in preventing future incidents. Is there a chance that the team member is simply modeling a specific leader? This is possible since some leaders achieved success through jerk-like behavior despite it.

Ignoring a jerk's lack of decency is not a viable option. Choosing to look the other way can be perceived as the company condoning the behavior. This may also be viewed as ignoring their responsibility. When jerk-like actions go unaddressed, team members may become hesitant to report future concerns. The cost of inaction can be significant, including increased turnover among key staff members. Silence is not a good option following the reporting or observation of poor behavior.

Maintaining team members' engagement and quality of their work must remain a priority. A culture where creativity and innovation are central to the organization's culture is where you should be working. Perhaps you have witnessed budgets blown and careers derailed due to inappropriate behavior from the front line to senior executive levels.

The choice is yours in taking an active or passive role to help mitigate the damage caused by jerks. Regardless of your position within your organization's hierarchy, taking steps to create and sustain a wonderful place to work is something you will look back on with pride. Building a bridge to help others overcome their unsuitable ways will also help you champion relationships, which in turn assists you in meeting your career objectives. By addressing jerk-like behavior and fostering a respectful environment, you contribute to a culture where everyone can thrive.

Point to Ponder: There is no such thing as having too much fulfillment at work. The level of your happiness is likely a result of how you are treated by others.

Question to Consider: To assist in creating a memorable impact on your colleagues and superiors, what actions can you take when witnessing inappropriate behavior?

_____

_____

_____

Backstabbing Brian

Backstabbing Brian may initially charm you with manipulation to make you feel comfortable, but his underlying intent is likely to drag you down to make himself look better. For him, betraying others and destroying someone's work may feel like recreation. His behavior may be rooted in jealousy, insecurity, or he just wants more attention. Protecting his own lies may be another motive for backstabbing, in the hope the truth will not surface. Spreading false rumors, degrading your work, and making derogatory remarks about you are never acceptable.

Brian's betrayals can catch you off guard, putting you in an embarrassing or difficult position. Undermining the high-quality work you perform to grow your career hurts and may incur negative consequences. Disrupting a department's momentum due to betrayal can set it back, potentially reducing the level of customer service or delaying the delivery of time-sensitive deadlines. Much of an organization's success requires commitments being executed and on time, which is never easy. Brian's interference reduces the synchronization needed to be able to compete successfully in the marketplace, as well as diminishing the level of employee engagement.

When dealing with a backstabber, carefully devise a clear strategy. Remaining calm and assessing the behavior objectively will keep you organized. Seeking support from key stakeholders including the Human Resources department and the backstabber's boss is a logical choice. When confronting the individual, have a direct conversation with them, offering details of why their behavior is concerning, including the damage it has created. As much as the person's behavior has upset you, avoid coming across as confrontational and do not engage in retaliation.

If Backstabbing Brian happens to be your boss, do not hesitate to address the problem he has created. He may have surrounded himself with others who support him and his inappropriate behavior, and being a boss may possess dedicated favorites within the organization. In such cases, it is wise to seek assistance from a Human Resources representative before taking any action. Determining who will address the behavior is a critical decision.

Are there actions you and your colleagues can take to prevent double-crossing within the organization? Yes, build strong relationships at work and squash false rumors immediately after they occur. Rise above this behavior and never engage in it yourself, while maintaining the level of professionalism you wish everyone to display. Compromising your own credibility and the team around you must be avoided at all costs, so never let negative behavior interrupt what is important. Finally, remember that for everyone who backstabs you, there are likely far more people who support you.

Point to Ponder: The enthusiasm you have for your career is vital and cannot be compromised. Never accept behavior that jeopardizes your credibility.

Question to Consider: What intentional strategies can you initiate to dissuade others from betraying yourself or your coworkers?

_____

_____

_____

Teflon Tom

Teflon Tom gets away with everything. Nothing sticks to this guy, and coworkers suspect he knows where "dead bodies are buried." This is code for knowing company secrets that would cause humiliation or legal trouble if specific information was publicized. Being a sole witness to the embarrassing conduct of a senior leader is a common suspicion of those perceived to be untouchable. People continue to wonder why he is that underperforming colleague which somehow stays on the payroll as if exempt from getting fired. And, Tom may realize the chance of long-term employment for doing little work remains strong.

This employee may have gone as far as charming executives into thinking he has tremendous potential or has misled them to believe he is a high performer. How about showing up for work on time? This may not appear to be important to Tom based on the way he perceives his level of "protection." Have you ever had a coworker who was related to a senior leader? Me too, in fact I have worked with several of them. In most instances the person's performance or conduct, or sometimes a lack of, became a popular discussion topic.

If you are one of Tom's coworkers, you may ask yourself how someone can get away with poor conduct. Does the term "double standard" come to mind? The untouchable employee may not be a bad person and in fact you might enjoy working with him. However, holding workers to different standards causes friction and needless distractions at work. You and your colleagues work hard to meet deadlines and help grow the business, and you appreciate the benefits and rewards that go along with success. Yet, a lack of fairness cannot be overlooked.

In the event you feel some colleagues are not being held to the same standards as you, do not let it frustrate you to the point where it impacts your performance, or how you feel about the company. Exercise caution in discussing your concerns with coworkers, as this may offer a negative perception of you. Instead, this is a good conversation to have with your boss or a member of the Human Resources department. Request that your conversation remain confidential, as there is a chance that your suspicions are not accurate, that the person may not actually be as protected as you may have thought.

It is natural to feel that certain employees benefit from "air-cover," a term utilized to infer someone is protected by high level leaders. When it comes to air-cover versus "contribution," continue to perform your best work. Strive to become known as a strong contributor and challenge undesirable interaction at work. This will assist in opening doors for you to be promoted faster than Teflon Tom.

Point to Ponder: If you want to grow, try not to become highly jealous of a colleague whose job security level does not make sense. Focus on doing the right things to make you shine.

Question to Consider: What can you do to ensure your hard work is seen and recognized on its own merits?

_____

_____

_____

Political Patty

Do you know someone at work who frequently blames every problem on a political party? Political bias has become much more rampant within the workplace, causing distractions which can be avoided. Working within companies will involve problems periodically, and possibly on a regular basis. This is to be expected. And there will always be those who find it appropriate to blame a political party. Is it possible the person is simply trying to make their own political affiliation look good and opposing ones look bad? This is possible, as we will never fully know someone's exact motives.

Partisan bitterness can pave the way toward a toxic work environment, as the concept of blaming anything or anyone is not healthy. Counterproductive behavior like this can stifle innovation, waste time and can unravel even the most productive teams. When workplace engagement is jeopardized, valuable work time can possibly be wasted, translating to an expense that may be difficult to recoup.

There will come a point when coworkers say, "enough is enough." When this happens, do not automatically assume the individual has an axe to grind against a political party. It may be just a symptom of the person feeling anguished about something occurring in their personal or professional life.

Make the time to meet with this person in a secluded setting and begin by asking how they feel about their current work and career situation. Give the individual the opportunity to explain any frustrations and let them vent. During the conversation, ask them if they are aware they have been blaming political organizations for problems that have occurred. The person may state they had no idea they were doing this. Regardless of their response, let the person know their actions have caused distractions within the work unit, then seek to understand their suggested solutions to stop this undesirable behavior as the next step. Taking no action is a poor option, especially if Political Patty is your boss, since inaction may lead to further unrest within the department.

Letting this behavior continue may be interpreted as the organization being perfectly okay with it. Make the time and effort to stop the political party blaming. Promoting a blame-free culture at your work is a good start to help avoid a negative work climate. Lead by example and hold people accountable for their actions and comments at work. Doing this will help ensure that Political Patty does not surface within your organization.

Point to Ponder: You may never fully understand someone who is overly motivated by politics. Regardless of one's political affiliation, blaming government activities for every mishap at work is inappropriate.

Question to Consider: How can you effectively reduce the number of work issues linked to non-corporate politics at your employer?

_____

_____

_____

Wesley The Weasel

Can you recall coworkers who take credit they did not deserve? Wesley the Weasel is notorious for doing this. He does not care much about you and may dedicate a portion of his time to digging up dirt on you and your colleagues. Does Wesley care much about the long-term success of the company? This scheming individual probably does not. When weasels remain on the payroll, one question to ask is whether they add value. While they may be a subject matter expert in one or more areas, a weasel's behavior can tarnish the engagement level of the people around them.

Senior weasels, who may be referred to as a "boss weasel," need to transform their behaviors. Someone focused solely on themselves sets a terrible example and does not help the company's culture. Company leaders must be role models for everyone under their umbrella of responsibility. If they are self-focused, they will see lesser results than someone who is team oriented.

You may never fully understand why weasels exist at work. You might find them to be insecure, and it is possible their supervisor is not giving them credit for the excellent work they perform. When you feel compelled to address the weasel's behavior, do not run away. Instead, focus on the facts and not your emotions, and never tell the person they are a weasel, as this could set them off. Explain to the person the conduct that concerns you and the harm it has caused. Do not take their past behaviors personally, simply move forward with the goal of helping the person exhibit a more acceptable behavior.

It is unlikely you will be exempt from witnessing weasel-like behavior at work. In fact, you should anticipate working with one or more of them again. As a preemptive strike, address this type of behavior sooner rather than later.

Modeling teamwork makes everyone around you feel important, and ensures credit is received where it is due. It seems obvious, but do not become a weasel yourself. In relation to current and future supervisors, do not work for a boss weasel whose improper demeanor cannot be repaired after multiple attempts. Your career is important, and you should be given every opportunity to become the best version of yourself. Again, ignoring a jerk's lack of decency is not a viable option.

Point to Ponder: It is important to distinguish a colleague dedicated to your success separate from someone who only cares about their own.

Question to Consider: What can you do to inspire others to make the entire team look good?

_____

_____

_____

Hollering Holly

Each of us has likely experienced working with or for a person who raises their voice frequently. Hollering Holly, whether she is your coworker or your boss, does not just raise her voice slightly louder than normal, she is a yeller. This type of behavior can be abusive and does not have to occur in today's climate, unless the person is notifying you that you are in immediate physical danger.

I think you would agree that not refilling the copy machine with paper does not constitute potential harm, and thus there is no need to yell at someone for it. Let's not forget about the email yeller, where the person occasionally utilizes all capital letters in a message filled with anger or tension.

When people become victims of yelling, the first emotions they experience are panic and fear. Being spoken to irrationally and in a raised voice hurts morale and productivity, and nobody should feel demeaned for their work. Is it possible that someone was the victim of a screamer after making a mistake? This is possible, but did the mistake cause the company to go out of business and the entire staff to be laid off? If not, it is just a mistake and figure out how to prevent it from happening again.

Holly may be a highly emotional person, or her shouting may be rooted in the culture of the company or her home life. There is a possibility that fear-based tactics and authoritarian leadership were cornerstones of the organization in its formative years. It is also possible that her boss is a yeller, and nobody has informed that person their behavior must change.

Dealing with the chronic yeller takes on different forms. If you are working for a "boss yeller," I recommend that you approach higher level management or Human Resources. Be confident they will outline a strategy to help your boss become more respectful.

Regardless of whether the person is your boss or not, when it comes to the time for you to confront the person it is important to remain calm and address the yelling in a private setting. Proceed to offer examples of their language and tone, but do not yell at the person, as fighting fire with fire may not help your cause. Often you will find the person admitting they yelled, apologizing, and explaining the root of why it happened, such as a personal problem occurring outside of work.

Creating and enforcing company programs like an anti-abuse policy and implementing training programs designed to aid in respectful behavior should be considered. Emotions will continue to run cold and hot, but it remains important that temper tantrums do not become common at work. Standing by and hoping the disrespectful behavior will fix itself is not a smart option, so I encourage you to invest in the right actions at the right time.

Point to Ponder: Do not waste your valuable time putting up with someone who yells at people. They are unfit to work at your employer and certainly have no business leading others.

Question to Consider: At what juncture will you tell a boss yeller either they leave the company or you do?

_____

_____

_____

Intimidating Ian

Do you remember the person at work who often humiliates, embarrasses, or frightens people, making others feel inferior? What about the coworker or boss who ridicules or makes unwarranted physical contact with others? Intimidating Ian's verbal abuse and emotional manipulation can create a form of control over others. Causing someone to feel needless insecurity or anxiety is not something that should be allowed or condoned.

Coercive actions can lead to a toxic workplace if left unchecked. You work hard and the same goes for your coworkers. When intimidating behavior surfaces, it reduces morale and productivity, interfering with the ability to move forward in your career. The instinct to raise your hand to take on more responsibility may be inhibited if you become a victim of corrosive behavior, since you may hesitate to increase your visibility. Employee creativity and innovation may also suffer when menacing occurs, thus inhibiting the company's ability to compete at a high level.

You can protect yourself and your team members from Ian. Your company has a vested interest in the well-being of its workforce, so do not tolerate any scare tactics. Instead, report them through the proper channels and be confident that your employer will help shield you from retaliation. You can bet the organization has policies in place to guard against unwanted behavior.

After dealing with the violator, help your employer take preventative action. Suggest that the open-door policy be clear to everyone. Periodic training for every leader and employee can serve as a strong reminder. Training venues can reinforce the behaviors that help companies meet their business objectives, while at the same time reminding staff of unacceptable behaviors, including intimidation.

Preventing a culture of local or company-wide intimidation is essential. Customer service, along with attracting and retaining talent are just some of the risks created by unnerving conduct. A culture of fear can never be tolerated, so you should expect to work in a climate where everyone is held accountable. Again, you work hard and aim to perform your best work. Do not let anyone deter you from accomplishing this.

Point to Ponder: There may be times you tell yourself the intimidating colleague will fix his inappropriate behavior himself. Be cautious about hoping this can be done without an intervention.

Question to Consider: What are you going to do when a coworker who is related to a senior company official intimidates you and others to get what he wants?

_____

_____

_____

Micromanaging Maria

If you resemble 99% of the workforce, you want trust and freedom to do your work independently, relying on a manager to provide guidance and support only when needed. As appropriate as that sounds, too often we find ourselves having to deal with a Micromanaging Maria.

Micromanagement is a style whereby a leader excessively controls their workers. They require frequent updates and will continually monitor your work. Telling their experienced employees exactly how to do things leaves little room for creativity and initiative. Micromanaging is sometimes referred to as an obsession instead of a management style.

This form of managing people is one of the worst inventions in the history of work. It drains morale and productivity, in addition to increasing staff turnover. Within work groups, it can easily create needless stress and burnout. No organization wishes employees to seek work elsewhere. However, talented people will continue to have career options. Going to another employer to reduce one's stress and regain the autonomy they once had will remain a possibility.

Why do managers feel the need to control their employees' work and decision making? It could be due to a lack of self-confidence, or the people who report directly to the micromanager have a stronger level of knowledge, skills, and abilities. The ability to delegate effectively may also be a true weakness for the individual. There is also a chance the micromanager is incorrectly placed in a leadership capacity. Perhaps the person was promoted simply based on their longevity within the company. Unfortunately, this does happen.

What do you do when you have to report to Micromanaging Maria, the "Boss Micromanager?" Fix her or run! Leave skid marks if you have to.

Someone who discourages independent decision-making may not be curable. Leaders are held responsible for creating an engaging work environment. However, those who choose to micromanage achieve the opposite.

When the micromanager is trying to exert excessive control over their people, this behavior is characterized as a "Category One" within the jerk-spectrum. (Category One is the worst kind). If you find that you happen to be a micromanager yourself, there is help for you.

Let go of the idea that each of your team members must be perfect and give them latitude within their work. Practice appropriate delegation skills to engage your employees and watch them become excited about reporting to work each day. Focusing on attaining results instead of the methods utilized will help you in your quest to become a stronger leader.

Point to Ponder: You determine your level of autonomy based on the performance and potential you demonstrate. Do not let a micromanager dictate every move you make.

Question to Consider: What initiative-taking steps can you take to show your boss there is no need to tell you what duties to perform or when to accomplish them?

_____

_____

_____

Pessimistic Pete

Numerous sayings have become popular at work over the course of history, i.e. "We can do this," or "We sure knocked that one out of the park." We cherish positive, optimistic language because this type of communication helps us strive to do even more. Unfortunately, we will witness unfavorable phrases, such as "that is never going to work," and "the boss won't go for it," spoken frequently by Pessimistic Pete. He is quick to point out potential faults in new ideas and seems to live to voice his complaints. Rarely are things good enough for pessimists, but unfortunately, we must collaborate with them.

In the presence of pessimists, other employees may hesitate to offer innovative ideas for fear they might be met with some unfair resistance. Causing conflict, draining energy from industrious staff members, and hurting the overall morale of the team may occur but it can also be prevented.

Pessimistic behavior will always be puzzling as to why it occurs. It is possible that some people resist change or are just not confident they can effectively solve problems. Opposing innovative ideas is also a method of keeping things in their current state. I do not believe that anyone wants to view everything in a negative fashion, as people may not realize they behave this way. You will encounter negative coworkers who simply have a blind spot, and often it is up to you to help pessimists overcome their undesirable communication style.

In dealing with chronically negative behavior, acknowledge the person's point of view and highlight their positive contributions. Listen in a non-defensive manner to understand if there are any obvious causes of their behavior and never single out the person in a group setting. Explain to the person how their behavior is being received at work and confirm their intentions. Show the person how their comments can become positive with just a few variations in their words.

Again, you will find yourself collaborating with pessimists during your career. My challenge to you is to not ignore their behavior, since doing so can continue to hurt you and your department's performance. Commit to helping the person become more positive. Being the person's ally will also reap benefits for you overall. Building a bridge to help someone overcome their inappropriate ways will also help you champion relationships to assist you in meeting your career objectives.

Point to Ponder: Be optimistic about your career. However, recognize you will be working with others who do not feel the same way.

Question to Consider: When reflecting on your upbeat, positive coworkers, what can you do to keep the pessimists from dragging down the teams' ideas?

_____

_____

_____

Two-Faced Timmy

Dependable coworkers who follow through with commitments are the people we count on at work. When a two-faced colleague changes their behavior based on the situation, it makes your job more difficult. Two-Faced Timmy may appear to be very cordial to you but may also paint you in a negative light when speaking to others. Is he really trying to turn people against you? This is possible, and if you have suspicions, you should try to confirm them. Although you may have a compact list of people at work you feel would never betray you, it can be surprising what people are capable of.

The root of two-faced behavior is not always clear. Some people are excessively childish, while others may just seek to fit in with as many coworkers as possible. Based on increasing workloads and tight deadlines, you do not need this level of distraction, nor do you need unnecessary stress in your life. Spreading false information infuriates even the most resilient team members. Productivity is important, and people want every opportunity to relax after leaving work at the end of each day.

The proper thing for you to do is have that tough conversation with your deceiving coworker. Do not seek revenge and maintain politeness but also be firm in stating facts and citing examples of how their behavior makes people feel. Help the person recognize their value to the team by pointing out clear strengths they demonstrate but stay on point to make it clear their behavior is unwanted. Your mission is to help the person admit their unbecoming ways, followed by their commitment to change. Do not let the person off the hook, get their commitment to improve and review their conduct regularly for an extended period.

Harmony at work is not a luxury you are guaranteed. You wish you could be nice and pleasant at work without exception each day. However, when you must deal with Two-Faced Timmy, you need to be assertive. Remember, you are not trying to fix his behavior just for your own sake. Your coworkers within the department also have no need for his insincere and dishonest style. Over the course of your career, you will discover how to perform your best work, even if it means helping someone overcome poor behavior.

Point to Ponder: Your most rewarding accomplishments are those attained with the help of trusted colleagues. When paired with a Two-Faced Timmy who does not complete what he commits to, you may not be turning out your best work.

Question to Consider: Which current or former coworker resembles Timmy? Assuming the person will be assigned to become your work partner long term, what are you going to say to them to ensure he does not betray you?

_____

_____

_____

Sherry Shirk

Have you ever wondered why you always honor and complete your work commitments, but cannot help but notice coworkers who avoid theirs? You recognize this person's name, it is Sherry Shirk, who dodges her responsibilities more often than you care to count. If you prefer terms like elude, evade, or sidestep, the result remains the same, the person is getting out of required duties which may impede your work.

Someone who needlessly increases the workloads of others, causing them to be overworked, is not someone you should tolerate. It may feel like the person is just being lazy, but creating longer working hours for others is not what you signed up for. Employee productivity and morale remain under a microscope at most organizations, with reliability being a key factor to remaining competitive. Have you ever experienced the loss of a customer? They have other service provider options and someone shirking their responsibilities can make the difference between retaining the customer and losing them to a competitor.

When the shirker's lack of timely execution impacts others, slows business performance, and damages their own reputation, you need to address the behavior. Seek to understand why the behavior is occurring first. It may be rooted in a lack of motivation, unfair expectations, insufficient performance feedback, or something outside of work.

Make sure your facts are accurate, as approaching the person may be sensitive. As always, when meeting with the person to express your concerns, where and when this occurs is important. Meeting the person in a public area or at 4:00 p.m. on a Friday afternoon is not appropriate. Your mission is to help the person understand that their work must be completed in a timely manner, and to get them to commit to doing so. It is obvious, but ensure the employee realizes they can count on you for support, and doing so will help build trust.

If shirking one's responsibilities become common within your work environment, your organization should initiate preventative measures. Regular performance feedback rhythms and creating a culture of accountability are important. Monitoring performance should never wait until formal evaluations are initiated; this should be an ongoing process. Nobody wants to see others be unsuccessful, so never delay in addressing the person who avoids their commitments.

Point to Ponder: Taking care of others may be something which is important to you. However, be prepared to address team members who do not take their responsibilities seriously.

Question to Consider: What specific actions can you take to energize others to become accountable for their duties?

_____

_____

_____

Potty Mouth Patrick

Profanity in the workplace, whether occurring in casual conversation or displaying anger, is a needless interruption. It does not matter who it comes from, obscene language is not welcome at work. Save it for your home if you feel compelled to use vulgar language. Common excuses, while useless, include not intending the vulgarity to be heard outside of the immediate conversation or not directed at any specific person.

Potty Mouth Patrick may be a likable person, but his swearing makes people feel uncomfortable, thus impacting work relationships and productivity. What about customer and client relationships? How much inappropriate language will they tolerate before shopping for a new partner? Not much. If by chance a client is the root of unprofessionalism at your workplace, now might be a suitable time to shop for a new client. You cannot afford to lose key employees because they dislike a client's inappropriate demeanor.

Why do people feel the need to use profanity? For those who think that dropping the "F-bomb" creates trust, this is misguided. Language utilized by professional comedians making their living with bad language will never go away. Movies can also push the envelope with curse words for some reason. However, our work environment requires a different language than that of comedians or movie dialogue, so it is important to separate both venues when it comes to acceptable language.

When Patrick's profanity becomes a problem, be confident you can get him back on course. Take a stand, reminding him that he is hurting others while doing no favors for himself. His vulgarity needs to stop. If you find the root of his obscenities stems from leadership levels above him, take a partner such as a senior leader or Human Resources member to fix the problem organization wide. As soon as you extinguish the potty mouth culture, ensure a zero-tolerance policy is implemented and adhered to. Now back to Patrick, give him the chance to grow his career once he proves he is a model citizen everyone appreciates again.

Point to Ponder: Too many people feel compelled to use profanity at work in hopes of creating a casual and friendly environment. This is unfortunate since inappropriate language can lead to lower employee and customer engagement.

Question to Consider: What are some things you can do to set the best possible example of professionalism and respect at work?

_____

_____

_____

Knee-Jerk Neil

Making decisions is never the easiest action you will perform at work. However, it is important to put an appropriate amount of thought into your decision before acting upon it. Knee-Jerk Neil reacts to situations without giving important components much thought or evaluating all the information related to it. Weighing each of the consequences involved can reduce the likelihood of slowing progress while compromising production and profitability. When decisions are made impulsively, a department or company's output may be jeopardized.

Organizations require leaders and decision-makers to operate swiftly, but some people make unusually quick decisions to enable the team to move on to other issues rapidly. However, work does not revolve around "moving stuff from the inbox to the outbox." It requires collaboration and buy-in when issues requiring a decision arise. There will also be leaders who come to a determination a little too quickly after getting excited about an idea.

Trying to change Knee-Jerk Neil is not an easy task. You do not want to stifle his initiative; you just want him to be conscious of his decision-making style. Do not think you can control this person. Instead, understand that you are there to influence him to do the right thing for all concerned. Remember that one of the best ways to influence others is to be an example. By not reacting with a gut reaction, you are modeling the right practice and can expect others to follow suit.

Knee-jerk decisions are often made by the involvement of one person. By bringing others into the fold, you increase the level of trust and teamwork, which is always critical within any organization. There are times when the pause button must be pushed, especially when a decision is being made with very little information at hand. Be the champion in teaching others the value of collaboration when decisions must be made. Being available to fully understand a situation improves one's decision-making capacity, resulting in the best possible outcome. Following this guidance to reduce spontaneous determinations will make you the leader people want to work for. As always, becoming a more effective leader will open career doors for you.

Point to Ponder: A sign of a great leader is how they involve others and consider multiple options when decisions must be made. How few decisions they make spontaneously can ultimately create more trust at work.

Question to Consider: Picture Knee-Jerk Neil working within your division at work. What can you do to inspire him to take more time and include others when decisions must be made?

_____

_____

_____

Kiss-Up/Kick-Down Kimberly

One of the challenges all leaders face is being both authentic and consistent in relationships with superiors and their subordinates. However, too many leaders fall into the unfortunate habit of flattering and offering extra support to those above them, while pressuring and belittling those who work for them. This is known as the kiss-up and kick-down style. As a leader, paying more attention to those above you, instead of dedicating your time to those who report to you may be a problem. However, with a change in mindset, they can get back on course.

The issues created by this unique style include increased turnover, a lack of employee commitment, and a reduction in employee engagement. A likely motive for this style is an attempt to speed up their career advancement. From a career trajectory perspective, this type of manager is potentially clouding their chances of moving up the organizational ladder. Promotions do not grow on trees, and this practice will limit Kimberly in her professional growth. Additionally, there are managers who do not manage the pressure of leading teams and delivering results. This may compel them to gush over senior leaders and be quick to blame their team members for department failures.

Working for or reporting to a kiss-up/kick-down manager is not the worst predicament to be in. However, someone needs to have a conversation with this person, helping them understand how this behavior is not a long-term solution for success. Considering the possibility that the person is unaware they are behaving in this manner, or they claimed it was how they were trained, be prepared to offer examples of how their behavior is causing a negative environment at work.

Converting this person to "kiss-down" instead of "kiss-up" will help them reach their career goals, while simultaneously increasing their level of career fulfillment, as well as yours. Remember that there are actions you can take after witnessing behaviors that burden you.

Point to Ponder: Cultivating an environment of fair and equal treatment is important within all levels of the organization. Unfortunately, reducing the level of upward favoritism is something you may have to deal with.

Question to Consider: What levels within the leadership hierarchy are you comfortable addressing when witnessing someone's kiss-up/kick-down style? Senior leaders? Middle managers? Peers?

_____

_____

_____

Authoritarian Arthur

Authoritarian Arthur, what a jerk. How can a leadership style made famous almost a hundred years ago exist today? An authoritarian leader forces absolute control over their subordinates, leaving almost no autonomy. People at work want their supervisor to trust them. However, authoritarians often feel their team members require close supervision for them to be efficient and effective. A lack of trust on the part of the leader is noticeably clear here. Obedience and adhering to completing work in the same tired manner are valued by Arthur much more than trust and engagement.

Nobody wants to work in a department or organization where there is no room for input or feedback. This can lead to worker aggression, increased turnover, and a reduction in motivation. People want to work in an environment where innovation is welcomed and expected. This creates the variety they need to perform their best work. A leader focusing purely on productivity, efficiency and operating results may require additional headcount, as some workers will not be inspired to meet or exceed their job duties.

The authoritarian style is the workplace equivalent of a fax machine. Any chance you have seen a fax machine lately? Seeing one is uncommon and there is not much use for them anymore. Considering the feelings of others is something that must remain top of mind for anyone in a supervisory role. This style does not take the feelings of others into account.

Dictatorial managers may believe that leaving people to work autonomously will not result in success for the worker or the department. Why do some leaders feel the need to manage people in this manner? It is possible that they might not have the confidence to empower others to work with the freedom their talents exhibit. So, compliment the boss when they do loosen the reins, and show them the benefit of doing so.

In the event you say to yourself that this boss will not change after efforts are made, and you can no longer tolerate their lack of trust, it may be time for you to move on. This is a final resort, but you need to remind yourself that meeting your professional goals and finding the career fulfillment you want is important to you.

Point to Ponder: You will meet authoritarian leaders who want to be effective, regardless of how they go about it. Make time to reevaluate your working environment when assigned to work for someone who does not trust you.

Question to Consider: What constructive advice might you give to your next coworker who states they hate working for an authoritarian leader?

_____
_____
_____

Condescending Connie

How do you want to be treated at work by others? For starters, you want it understood that you are capable and smart. Condescending Connie talks down to others, often belittling them. Correcting people frequently in a patronizing tone and portraying an attitude of superiority is another attribute of unwanted, condescending behavior. Once someone is fully trained in their role, continuing to reiterate instructions on how to perform basic functions becomes unnecessary.

Productive work involves teamwork and the execution of tasks with innovation sprinkled in. A person undermining the confidence of coworkers has the potential to create an unproductive working climate, and an overcorrecting colleague can leave you feeling frustrated and disrespected. So why does a person behave this way? It is possible the person has a blind spot and does not intend to harm anyone. It is also possible that their current or former supervisor modeled this type of behavior.

At some point, you or someone within the department needs to help your condescending colleague or boss change from this undesirable behavior. Be cautious in responding to Connie using the first method that comes to mind. Instead, use your corporate filter and remain composed. While keeping the conversation calm and professional, inform the person of the impact their actions have caused. Also, help the person understand that everyone wants to do their best work in a positive, team-oriented culture. This conversation should not become confrontational, especially since the person may not be aware of how they are treating others.

To create a workplace where people are excited to show up each day, catch early signs of undesirable conduct and address them quickly before they become a habit. Remember to treat others the way they want to be treated.

Point to Ponder: Career expectations include working with respectful people. Your coworkers will agree with this, but do not leave it up to them to take action when inappropriate behavior exists.

Question to Consider: How long will you work for a condescending boss before you speak up? One year? One month? One week? One hour?

_____

_____

_____

Billy the Bully

Do you remember the schoolyard bully growing up? A pretty mean kid with the potential of you being bruised after school? Well, workplace bullying is different, as physical pain is rarely part of this conduct. Instead, Billy the Bully creates emotional disturbances by degrading, offending, or humiliating someone or a group of workers. Delivering unwarranted criticism or blame has no place at work. Aggression and threats, whether physical or psychological, can be construed as abuse, and cannot be tolerated by colleagues or supervisors.

A typical workplace has varying levels of stress and anxiety simply by the nature of work itself. When your self-esteem and confidence are negatively impacted due to being mistreated, both you and the employer suffer. You want to grow within your career and your company needs you to perform your best work, enabling it to remain competitive. High turnover coupled with a damaged reputation is a position your employer can avoid with proper interventions.

Whether annoying conduct is either accidental or intentional, seek to understand the root cause, but do not feel compelled to spend too much time on this. The workplace bully is most interested in their own success, instead of everyone in the department becoming a winner. Addressing this type of behavior is not optional, someone needs to act swiftly, and involving Human Resources or a senior leader is highly recommended in advance of meeting with the individual.

One of the keys to remaining in business revolves around the collective performance of its employees. You and your colleagues want to work in conditions which remain fair and respectful, thus be mindful to recognize coworkers who you suspect are in distress. Words of your support to an anguished coworker can be very meaningful to them.

Remember that a person can ruin your day in sixty seconds or less, but they have no right in doing so. Again, do not hesitate to take action when someone shows aggression toward any members within your sphere of influence.

Point to Ponder: Having fun at work and achieving fulfillment should not be saved for later. Anyone causing excessive stress must change, and if the person refuses, they need to change employers.

Question to Consider: What steps can you take to ensure the company bully never gets a second chance to remain on the team?

_____

_____

_____

Sabotage Sally

Someone ruining your day in sixty seconds or less often comes as a complete surprise. Is it possible this can happen from someone you least expect? Sabotage Sally can stop you from achieving something that might be your best work. In addition to taking credit for your ideas and excluding you from important communication, a coworker taking deliberate action to discredit you is not welcome at work. Whether the person is your boss or a colleague, criticizing or belittling you, or interfering with your reputation is not something you should tolerate.

You have worked hard to build strong relationships with people who count on you. With saboteurs lurking within your department, the team may not be able to meet important deadlines. Additionally, messing with your stress and confidence hurts your ability to be successful.

Have you ever wondered why people feel the need to hinder someone's work? The person may not be managing pressure well and may feel their own job is at risk. Others may feel the need for revenge or are simply jealous of others' success.

Regardless of why someone feels the need to sabotage someone else's work, they must be stopped. Deliberately damaging someone's work cannot be allowed to occur, so create a plan to deal with the person. Address the offender, being firm while providing examples.

Again, this behavior would not likely support any organizational value related to teamwork. Get the person to commit to changing and later call out positive behaviors when they occur to let them know they are improving. At the same time, continue to perform your best work and set the example you intend everyone else should follow.

Point to Ponder: Every significant accomplishment should result in you receiving credit. However, it is important to remember there are others out there eager to take away your praise.

Question to Consider: What is holding you back from addressing the actions of coworkers who sabotage others' work, who also finds nothing wrong in damaging a person's reputation?

_____

_____

_____

Arrogant Andy

The concept of one's self-worth is important, but when a person thinks too highly of themselves and proceeds to act selfishly, the local team can suffer. Someone at work being self-centered and often immature are characteristics of someone you may not want to be around. Arrogant Andy can be a nice person in general, but his feeling of superiority may give him a sense of entitlement, potentially leading to toxic relationships. You have seen colleagues earn promotions in the past, but hopefully it was due to their performance and potential, not boasting or trying to show others they are always right.

Have you ever stopped to evaluate how a team became strong? One of the competencies needed to accomplish this is humility. Arrogant people can make others feel undervalued, leading to a reduction in morale. Colleagues who frequently take over conversations and meetings can create tension and harm innovation is another sign.

A divided team is rarely a successful one, and people being afraid to admit their mistakes may contribute to an incompetent team. The "show off" at work may not understand how they are coming across, or it is possible the person simply believes their way is the best or only way of doing things.

Help change the conceited individual by offering constructive feedback in a private meeting, explaining how their behavior makes others feel. Compliment their eagerness to be successful, but offer preferred ways of achieving success.

Do not feel compelled to search the company handbook for a rule against arrogance, because you will probably not find one. Instead, create an atmosphere of humility where everyone can do their best work, helping to retain the most talented employees who actively praise one another.

Point to Ponder: Model the behavior you expect, lodged in humility. When colleagues display a sense of superiority and immaturity, try a little harder to help them get back on track.

Question to Consider: How many arrogant employees can you reasonably tolerate within your department? Two? One? None? What might you do to help them act sincerely and dedicated to the team?

_____

_____

_____

Manipulating Molly

Have you taken the time recently to evaluate what you want from your boss and coworkers? Dignity, respect, and support to create your best work? As reasonable as this sounds, Manipulating Molly may not be helping your cause. Someone who misrepresents information and who does not hesitate to exploit others to make themselves look better has no place on your team. Whether the person is guilt-tripping, pitting one employee against another, or spinning facts, the well-being of you and your colleagues should not be compromised.

Working conditions do not dictate that someone has ultimate control over you in your work. Trust is something that cannot be negotiated, and undermining others hurts the level of enthusiasm and drive to accomplish the organization's objectives. Commanding the way meetings and conversations occur does not inspire people to work with an innovative mindset and potentially impedes the corporation's ability to get ahead. Again, employee engagement and the potential for turnover cannot be allowed to suffer because of deceitful conduct at work.

Someone must address the "masters of the mind game" if not yourself. Regardless of their motives, help them understand that honesty and looking out for others is key to success. Set clear expectations and do not focus on blaming the person. Instead, help Molly know how you feel and stop short of the temptation to simply ignore her.

If you elect to address this unwanted behavior yourself, take a day to determine how you go about it since the first method you consider may not be the best one. While Molly may not admit any faults, let her know that it is alright to express her mistakes and failures, citing nobody is perfect.

When addressing the person's behavior, remember not to give in to their manipulations. From a prevention standpoint, do your part in helping to build trust, sincerity, and fairness. Your efforts in advocating for a team-first environment will reap benefits for you and your employer.

Point to Ponder: Take charge of the freedom and autonomy you have earned. Nobody is allowed to take this away from you.

Question to Consider: In pursuit of continuing the vocational duties you love performing, which current colleagues do you trust partnering with to address Manipulating Molly's corrosive behavior?

_____

_____

_____

Obnoxious Olivia

You have witnessed inappropriate and offensive behaviors during your career. Fortunately, you have also worked alongside very polite, well-mannered colleagues. Think back to the ones you preferred not to be around. Where does Obnoxious Olivia fall into that spectrum? You know, the person who talks loudly and does not hesitate to interrupt you, and is not concerned with negating what someone else has to say? This person can also make abusive comments and insists on having the last word in all conversations.

Your spirit at work can affect your performance and your potential to move to higher levels in the organization. You may also dread going to work knowing that your impolite boss or colleague has no concept of "please" or "thank you."

Your productivity may not meet or exceed expectations when surrounded by people making insensitive, uncaring comments. Reasons for this behavior may include unresolved issues, eagerness to gain attention, or simply seeking to gain more power. Regardless of the reasons, the climate you work in is important and the obnoxious habits of others should not be tolerated.

While the person demonstrating uncivilized behavior may not be aware of the disruption they cause, do not take the chance that it will go away on its own. Minimizing your contact with a graceless person is not a preferred option nor a smart long-term solution. Confront the person and help them understand the unpleasant atmosphere they are creating. Share examples that concern you and explain how their lack of sensitivity is not helping their career trajectory. Standing up for yourself by providing constructive criticism about their annoying behavior will go a long way.

The word "suffer" is not a common term used at work, but in this case do not hesitate to stress its importance when dealing with an obnoxious boss or colleague.

Point to Ponder: At the end of one's life, nobody wants "Obnoxious" inscribed on their headstone. Consider taking one for the team by correcting abusive and uncivilized behavior before a person earns a nickname they might later regret.

Question to Consider: You want to work in a culture steeped in respect. How will you approach your boss to help them after they are branded rude, crude, or obnoxious?

_____

_____

_____

Secretive Sarah

Transparency is something you want and expect. You make the effort to keep everyone informed and in the loop, which creates trust and makes people feel important. This is noble, but Secretive Sarah does not follow your lead. A boss or colleague not sharing vital information about strategy or goals, or even changes within your department is not helping the team's cause. People who guard information too closely, especially when it comes to making decisions, are not utilizing the collective wisdom and talents available within the company.

You have worked diligently to move up during your career, accepting more responsibility. Your level of trust within your department and company may be up for grabs when issues needing your involvement are kept from you and your coworkers. This can hurt morale and the unified team you belong to. Feeling left out is a sensitive issue, especially when learning your input would have been valuable given the opportunity to contribute. It is unfortunate, but some decision making occurs without involving others to avoid resistance of a specific person's agenda.

To prevent eroding trust, help your employer recognize the talent of the workforce, while at the same time reminding them that covert decision making and withholding information are not helping meet its objectives. At the very least, sharing information can reduce the likelihood of duplicating efforts.

Tight-lipped bosses may feel that withholding information makes them more important and exerts more control over their team members. I would challenge that their level of importance should come from the admiration of those who work for them. Their image can be enhanced by sharing information with those associated with the issue in an open and honest workplace. Remember, you always have a say when it comes to sustaining the right working climate, one where team members feel appreciated and empowered.

Point to Ponder: The level of what you deliver is highly dependent on receiving the most accurate information available. Unfortunately, remain aware that one or more coworkers may withhold facts and figures from you.

Question to Consider: What work habits do you utilize to ensure you are apprised of pertinent information at work? And how would you detect someone not sharing valuable knowledge and details with others?

_____

_____

_____

Dirty-Look Dan

Communicating with others at work takes on multiple methods, obviously some will be written while others verbal and non-verbal. Each day you will come across a high number of coworkers and you are required to interpret their facial expressions. Your hope is that you find each one to be pleasant and enjoyable, but then you cross paths with Dirty-Look Dan. Working with someone who frequently displays an angry and disapproving look can ruin your mood rapidly. Additionally, there will be times when you feel guilty thinking you did something wrong, or the person may make you feel embarrassed while in the company of others.

Increasing one's stress and anxiety levels can deteriorate morale. The relationships that you have worked so hard to build can be negatively impacted after piercing stares are directed your way. By the time you finish reading this book, you may not see this behavior as the worst of the bunch. However, your colleagues or boss giving you the evil eye must be addressed. Do not revise your resume or leave skid marks and try not to let it impact your performance. Frankly, I think you can fix this one.

Try to understand what the person was doing immediately prior to delivering dagger eyes your way. Had the person just met with their boss or are there any patterns in the occurrences? It might not be you that the person is hostile towards but meet with the person to address how you perceive their facial expressions. Also, consider asking a highly trusted colleague to listen to your description of the person's frowns and scowls.

Remain confident in your ability to deal with this person. Ignoring the problem is not a remedy. Lastly, "look in the mirror" to ensure the person is not simply returning the same inappropriate expressions that you may unknowingly be giving them.

Point to Ponder: Working hard to please others is important, and in exchange you expect to receive glances that appear to be pleasant. When the opposite occurs, seek to understand how a Dirty-Look Dan surfaced.

Question to Consider: What specific changes or improvements would you suggest in helping to reduce the level of negativity or anger within your current department?

_____

_____

_____

Confrontational Cathy

Have you ever worked with someone where productive and harmonious conversations were not the norm? You know, the type of coworker who is set on making you feel inferior? Confrontational Cathy has rough edges to say the least, with her unofficial nickname being "Gotcha." People dominating conversations can occur regularly. We have come to expect this. However, initiating arguments and making personal attacks on others cannot be accepted.

Collaborating with a combative boss or colleague creates unnecessary pressure on you, affecting the quality of your work. Every vocation requires concentration and focus, and unfortunately there will be times when you collaborate with contentious people. Does your ability to provide the best possible product or service to your customer or client suffer when dealing with offensive team members? Yes, this is highly possible. Belligerent conduct may be the result of someone's anger or inability to perform their job. It is also possible that the person is highly competitive but cares little about the welfare of others.

You need to address this antagonistic behavior, as there is no place for it at work. Initiating a private conversation with this type of jerk may feel a little daunting, so seek counsel if needed to help you prepare. Try to understand what is driving their behavior such as any unique values or beliefs but do not cave to any excuses, since nobody wants to work in a toxic environment.

After dealing with the behavioral issue, you will find that the department gladiator's commotion and comments reflect on themselves, and not you.

Building a bridge to help this person will contribute to your reputation as the all-star employee everyone strives to be. In the end, the working conditions are better because of you.

Point to Ponder: Before committing to your next career move, validate the team members within the work group being supportive and not putting unnecessary pressure on others.

Question to Consider: Reflecting on your current and past work environments, how has Confrontational Cathy's antagonistic behavior been derailed? Would you have taken a different approach?

_____

_____

_____

Nasty-Gram Nate

Take a moment and remember that recent email you received where you were commended for outstanding work, leadership, or both. You know the one where your peers and superiors were copied. I am confident you felt gratified and special. Now go ahead and reflect on the one you or your coworkers received from Nasty-Gram Nate, the one that was full of criticism, potentially insulting to the recipient and copied some of your peers and superiors. Communication written with hostility or sarcasm, intended to tear someone down, must be eliminated.

Mean-spirited messages create needless strain within your working climate. You have told yourself that your best work be completed in surroundings where people remain polite and want the organization to be successful. Receiving "job-angry" emails hurts the level of engagement, wastes time, and creates unnecessary distractions within a department. These documents may result from an overreaction on the sender's part or simply venting frustrations. Neither of these motives is considered noble, and the sender needs to be dealt with.

When you receive these types of messages, regardless of whether they are sent from your boss or a peer, I do not recommend initiating an email reply, especially one using the "reply all" feature. Address the problem first by meeting with the sender. You can cover yourself later, which may be handled by the sender retracting their message and apologizing to you and the others copied.

Let the person know your side of the story and remind them of your dedication and competence. Also, explain how their message has created potential damage to your reputation as well as staining their own image.

Your prime objectives are to sustain a supportive and respectful working relationship with Nate and preserve your character. Helping him improve his diplomacy benefits him and further enhances your reputation.

Point to Ponder: Offensive written language cannot be confused with messages that are intended to be direct. Hostile communication landing with the force of a cannonball cannot be condoned.

Question to Consider: What is more concerning to you, the language utilized in an inappropriate message or the people who were copied on it? How many chances are you going to give Nasty-Gram Nate to stop making offensive comments in his written correspondence?

_____
_____
_____

Rumor Mill Roger

Wasting your valuable time addressing distractions at work is common. Have you ever wondered how much of your time has been consumed by listening to rumors? How about the amount of time you have spent trying to dispel them? Rumor Mill Roger may be a fun and talented colleague, but his efforts need to focus more on his work. In many cases, he appears to originate most if not all the rumors within the department.

While some comments may seem simple and initiated for the sake of fun, circulating unwarranted gossip can harm someone's reputation. Leaking inaccurate information can also lower morale, creating demotivated team members.

Trust is never easy to build, and the department "big mouth" disrupts the ability of the business to meet its goals. Some people spread rumors because they feel it might improve working relationships. Others might do the same because they believe it might increase their own stature at work. Roger may think it is funny, but it is not, what he does not realize is that his efforts may jeopardize his own integrity.

You may have little hope that this behavior can be stopped. However, eliminating needless gossip that hurts people at work must be addressed. Consider validating your feelings with your boss or a trusted coworker, then decide how and who will take the lead. When meeting with Roger, share evidence traced back to him and the harm he has caused. He needs to be reminded that he, as well as others, have professional goals and spreading rumors will not benefit anyone's career. Eliminating rumors at work will give you back time and energy previously spent dealing with unnecessary gossip, so do not sit back on this one. The level of gratitude you seek from your career should never be compromised or interrupted.

Point to Ponder: Offering constructive suggestions to coworkers should include the need to focus on their own job duties instead of creating or relaying gossip which benefits nobody.

Question to Consider: What can you say to colleagues to inspire them to voice praise for others instead of circulating information that may hinder someone's passion to succeed?

_____

_____

_____

Terrible Tara (Bonus Jerk)

Over the past twenty-five chapters, you have been introduced to jerks and their jerk-like behavior. During one or more chapters, you may have thought about a boss or coworker who demonstrated that particular chapter's specific behavior, and the same person came to mind during an additional chapter. I refer to this person as a "double jerk." That type of working relationship is unfortunate; however, things could be worse. Let me introduce you to Terrible Tara, a "triple jerk" who displays three or more of the twenty-five offensive behaviors we have described in this journey together.

Identifying a combination of three jerk styles can take on a multitude of forms. Here are examples:

- Hollering, Intimidating, and Micromanaging Tara
- Backstabbing, Pessimistic, and Condescending Tara
- Authoritarian, Manipulating, and Confrontational Tara
- Obnoxious, Secretive, and Arrogant Tara

You can consider each of those examples a "triple jerk," but let's call this situation what it is. The person's behavior is terrible, and I hope you do not have to work for or with anyone whose conduct resembles that magnitude. Another image you may be thinking about is a "past Tara" whom you learned to tolerate. No more tolerating, you should be eager to "celebrate" everyone around you. You should view this person as a personal challenge, one where you tell yourself that you can help them with the necessary repairs.

In addressing the triple jerk, evaluate their level of jerk-like behaviors. The person may be a "minor jerk" in one or more characteristics, and the

53

same goes for the "major jerk" level. Someone who has reached major jerk levels in three styles is much more offensive than their counterpart displaying three minor jerk level characteristics. Some behaviors may be considered more offensive than others. For example, you may be able to handle an arrogant person more easily than someone who backstabs you.

After sizing up the challenge at hand, you are wise to take a partner, sharing your perceptions and validating that Tara's behavior must be addressed. How this person is approached can be highly situational. Determining who will meet with the person could include someone who has helped them improve in the past, like their supervisor, a senior leader, Human Resources, or a combination of each. You are not seeking to help the triple jerk turn around solely for your benefit. You are doing this for the sanity of the staff, the organization, and the person themself.

Point to Ponder: Avoiding people who fit the triple jerk level will not cure their issues. For the sake of your own career satisfaction as well as others, pull out all the stops to help this person turn around sooner rather than later. You will find the benefits significant.

Question to Consider: How can you stay focused at work when Terrible Tara's multiple unruly behaviors remain in your department?

_____

_____

_____

Jerk Prevention Strategies and Techniques

The previous twenty-six chapters identified and addressed fictitious characters who displayed inappropriate, jerk-like behavior. You have learned the impact of jerk behavior and why people might behave in one or more of those disrespectful fashions. This book also emphasized the reasons why the behavior must be addressed, how you can take action, and when to seek assistance when dealing with a jerk.

Each of these insights and activities remains important in creating a respectable work environment. However, dealing with bad behavior as it occurs will not be enough. The prevention strategies and techniques your organization enlists will be critical to achieving a great workplace.

The term "zero-tolerance" is frequently stated but not always utilized. Your employer should not tolerate inappropriate behavior. It must make it highly apparent which types of behavior are the most concerning. Here are preventative actions you and your organization can initiate in its quest to make your workplace as jerk-free as possible:

- Institute the "No Jerk Rule." No explanation is required.
- Conduct three times as many stay interviews as exit interviews.
- Model the right conduct, showing everyone is respected.
- Create safe and anonymous reporting channels.
- Protect whistleblowers and pursue claims of retribution.
- Provide refresher courses on respectful behavior regularly.
- Reinforce the company's mission, vision, and values.
- Hold each employee accountable, every day.
- Distribute *The One-Minute Jerk at Work* to each employee.

These preventative assignments are not all-inclusive. Just like no two organizations are identical, the right strategies and techniques will vary. I recommend a "one-size-fits-one" approach when it comes to the actions a company employs to create an environment where people are excited to report to work each day. Schedule guest speakers to help reinforce your organization's expectations, since hearing the message from the same leader every year becomes less effective.

Again, lead with prevention. Do you know who is ready and willing to assist your organization with installing appropriate jerk-prevention strategies and techniques? Yes, it is me, Rich Salon, aka Rich-The-HR-Guy. It has been my privilege to perform critical employee relations work for leading companies, and I would be thrilled to meet you. You can reach me at **Rich@RichTheHRGuy.com** and I commit to providing remedies to your company in its quest to become and remain jerk-free.

Point to Ponder: Problem behavior does not fix itself. Enlist the help of coworkers when installing prevention strategies designed to create the jerk-free environment you seek.

Question to Consider: When planning to initiate techniques to dissuade employees from demonstrating shoddy work habits, what resistance do you expect to encounter? What will you do to negate any resistance that surface?

_____

_____

_____

AFTERWORD

It only takes one jerk to ruin a team and its dream.

- R.T.H.R.G.

I hope this book has inspired you to never settle when it comes to your career. Give yourself the chance to find the level of happiness you have only dreamed about, the one where jerk-like behavior rarely surfaces. In finding your own fulfillment, assist others to do the same by promoting a respectful and courteous climate. There will be times when you must help coworkers overcome unruly behavior, this is expected. When this happens, you will find that you grow professionally because of how you dealt with the issue.

Use the insights within this book to remain unleashed and trust yourself to look out for your employer. An organization's ability to compete in the marketplace does not occur by accident. It takes everyone living its mission, vision, and values to remain in business. An organization that does not correct jerk-like behavior may not survive. The people within your workplace may not have the talents or the confidence to call out disruptions, so model the important competency we call "taking action."

Seek to understand the level of empowerment you are afforded within your employer as to how to diffuse jerks. Dealing with jerks consumes valuable time and reminds you that you can make an impact on the satisfaction level of yourself and the others around you. While there are no guarantees you will work in a setting where harmony is the norm, tell yourself that you will do your part in contributing to the best possible conditions.

The only benefit to jerk-like behavior at work is increased job security for us Human Resources professionals. In speaking for myself and my HR peers, we would gladly give up that unique advantage to witness a more positive, respectful, and supportive climate.

You should consider installing the "no jerk rule" at work, and if you need more insights on this, please contact me. It is important to remember if any behavior you witness or learn about has the potential to result in violence at work, contact your manager or a senior leader immediately to help minimize the likelihood of physical danger.

Now, about the quotes throughout the book. I suspect you found them unfamiliar. You might also be curious as to the author of these quotes, the person using the acronym "R.T.H.R.G." For those of you who have not figured out the origin of that acronym, it stands for **Rich-The-HR-Guy.** Yes, it is me. That is my long-term nickname.

Imagine what your life would be like if you rarely had to deal with a jerk at work and the job duties you perform created more happiness than you ever expected. When this occurs, please congratulate yourself on being in the right opportunity and enjoying the career fulfillment you seek. Do not waste another moment, that level of fulfillment is waiting for you. Just do not let any jerks interrupt you.

I wish you all the best.

ABOUT THE AUTHOR

Jerks are like a bouquet of poison ivy.

- R.T.H.R.G.

Rich Salon is a Human Resources and Employee Relations expert. His professional purpose is to help people find career fulfillment. He helps leading companies improve the critical employment experience for staff members at all levels. Most people know him as Rich-The-HR-Guy. He is also a Career Transition Coach, where he helps match people to business ownership opportunities through his own company, Business Ownership Connection, LLC. He is a single source for all matters relating to careers, assisting career seekers in the areas of employment, consulting, and business ownership.

Career highlights and recognition include being named "Hero of the Economy" by a major news network for work performed at a former employer and being nicknamed "Chief Engagement Officer" at another. There is one aspect of his career that Rich is eager to forget. He has been part of project teams at multiple corporations who have laid off corporate and field team members, with the work of these teams resulting in job losses of over 11,000 members. Rich has been fortunate to offset this devastation by making a positive impact on the careers of a similar magnitude.

Rich has a passion for public speaking. He enjoys speaking on a multitude of topics including career fulfillment, corporate culture, employee engagement, and career transition. When Rich is not giving back to others while at work, he is giving back to others after work. He has been a proud member of Rotary International since 2015, where he continues to serve in multiple leadership capacities, helping to drive membership-related activities for clubs located in Pennsylvania through South Carolina.

For further inspiration in taking your career to the next level, consider purchasing Rich's first book, *Career Trust: Fifty-Two Doses of Reality To Help You Find Career Fulfillment*, or his second one, *Unleashing Your Career: Thirty-One Insights Devoted To Your Professional Journey.* You know where to find it, the same place you purchased *The One-Minute Jerk at Work.*

What is in store for Rich's future? Bestselling author. This is where your friends and colleagues come in. You know where to buy this book. Please inspire them. Also, Rich will continue his work as "The Jerk Authority" through his work in Human Resources and as a Keynote Speaker since people at all levels can experience a higher level of fulfillment with fewer jerks in the workplace.

Feel free to contact Rich Salon at (804) 385-1309 or by his email address at Rich@RichTheHRGuy.com.

ACKNOWLEDGEMENTS

Jerks love to play. However, there may come a time when
they need to find another team to play on.

- R.T.H.R.G.

The inspiration of this book came from a multitude of people in my life. First, I want to thank my wife and children, Laura, Cory, and Mary, who believed that my purpose in life is to help others, even at the expense of extremely long hours while working in corporate America.

To my parents, Elene, RaNae, and Robert Salon, for inspiring me to be the best version of myself and never portraying life as anything more complicated than taking care of others.

I want to thank each of the editors of this book, Alan, Andy, Bonnie, Brenda, Chris, Duane, Ed, Laura, Lynn, Mary, Peter, Scott, Steve, and another Steve. Each of them offered me their valuable time and provided candid feedback and helpful suggestions.

My profound gratitude goes out to former Human Resources and Employee Relations mentors for helping me learn throughout my career, while allowing me to do more than I ever thought I could accomplish. This enabled me to make our companies better and increase the career satisfaction to large employee populations.

To my terrific mentors within Rotary International. Thank you for having confidence in my leadership and affording me challenging assignments. I credit my experience in Rotary International to inspiring me to become a wish-granter for adults diagnosed with a terminal illness following my retirement. I am doing this in loving memory of my mother, Elene Salon.

CALL TO ACTION

Do not let jerks derail your sanity.

- R.T.H.R.G.

The insights gained throughout this book must result in you taking action when necessary. Challenge yourself to not settle when witnessing or learning about inappropriate behavior. If you feel that you may not have the confidence to address jerks, take a partner who may be a colleague or a senior leader. The choice will remain yours in taking an active or passive role to help mitigate the damage caused by jerks, so make the effort to choose the right path.

One of the best lessons you can take away from this book is the importance of reminding yourself of what you want from your work. This likely includes dignity and respect, which you are entitled to regardless of who your employer is.

Please utilize the reflections area beginning on page 67, the first one titled "The Most Challenging Jerk I Need to Help Change." Use these pages as a worksheet to plan how you are going to deal with specific jerks as they surface, or how you will make changes within yourself. In the event the content of this book has led to a change in how you manage offensive behavior, I would love to hear from you. Please send me a note about your situation to Rich@RichTheHRGuy.com.

If you are a senior Human Resources leader currently employed by an organization, you can consider replacing the employee handbook with *The One-Minute Jerk at Work*. Your company's handbook may include almost every action a team member can take to be fired, which some people might find valuable. However, your employee's understanding of what jerk-like behavior looks like and arming them with the inspiration contained in this book can create a more effective organization.

I remain enthusiastic about helping people, organizations, and associations improve their workplace climate. Also, helping people nationwide with their career search is something I continue to do. If you need assistance in your professional journey, please call on me, I am happy to help you. Whether you give this book to a friend or colleague, please stay in touch with me.

Regarding yourself, friends, colleagues, or your boss, I am happy to help in managing conduct which has created tension, pressure, or anxiety. My career purpose is to help people find the level of career fulfillment they want, and someone working in the presence of a jerk can compromise the likelihood. Just send me an email with a request. Lastly, do not become a jerk, you will not like how it fits.

NEED A SPEAKER?

Jerks are the equivalent of your worst Monday. Fix them

and spare yourself from bad days.

- R.T.H.R.G.

I hope you enjoyed reading *The One-Minute Jerk at Work*. If I can assist an organization you are acquainted with by speaking about workplace engagement and multiple career-related topics, please contact me at Rich@RichTheHRGuy.com. I help leading companies improve their employee experience, resulting in a higher level of career satisfaction for staff members at all levels.

Here is a sample of my speaking topics:

- The One-Minute Jerk at Work
- Moving from Employee Engagement to Career Fulfillment
- Company Culture: The Secret Sauce
- Leaving Skid Marks – Sure Fire Ways to Increase Resignations
- Avoid Pencil-Whipping Your Employees Growth
- Build Your Brand by Taking Care of Others
- Unleashing Your Career to Discover Fulfillment
- Career Transition – Always Prepared for Your Next Move

The Most Challenging Jerk I Need to Help Change

_____

_____

_____

_____

_____

_____

_____

The Easiest Jerks for Me to Address

_____

_____

_____

_____

_____

_____

_____

Changes I will Make to Avoid Becoming a Jerk

_____

_____

_____

_____

_____

_____

Jerks I Will Never Tolerate Again

_____

_____

_____

_____

_____

_____

70

Jerks I will Always Seek Assistance Prior to Addressing

Jerk Behavior Deemed Acceptable to My Employer

Boss Jerks I Commit to Help Change

_____

_____

_____

_____

_____

_____

Jerk Survey: The Most Common Jerk at My Employer

_____

_____

_____

_____

_____

_____

Jerks I Will Avoid

_____

_____

_____

_____

_____

_____

Jerks I Can Work Around

_____

_____

_____

_____

_____

_____

Direct Report Jerks I Will Address More Assertively

_____

_____

_____

_____

_____

_____

_____

The Biggest Jerk During My Career

_____

_____

_____

_____

_____

_____

_____

NOTES

NOTES

NOTES

NOTES

NOTES